GW01099481

THE WHISPERS SERIES

'THIS IS FOR YOU, MUM!'

by Lynn Massey-Davis
Illustrated by Louise Barton

Nightingale

An imprint of Wimbledon Publishing Company
LONDON

Copyright © 2000
Illustrations © 2000 WPC

First published in Great Britain in 2000
by Wimbledon Publishing Company Ltd
P.O. Box 9779 London SW19 7ZG
All rights reserved

First published 2000 in Great Britain

ISBN: 1903222 22 2

Produced in Great Britain
Printed and bound in Hungary

Dedication:

"From me to my mum,
Now I'm one too
Were you once me,
Or did I become you?"

There is so much written about mothers by adults, both from an intellectual and analytical stand point, sometimes looking back in anger. We also spend time as adults remembering our own childhood and what it felt like to us. All of these perspectives are dulled by time and have lost their freshness and immediacy.

As I muddled through my mornings from hell, I wondered how my children saw me. Did they see this confused person, trying to juggle home, work, kids husband, dogs, cats etc... or did they see something else?

The answer came loud and clear when my daughter, then six, brought some work home from school. It was a piece about some marvellous, miraculous person who had achieved so much - as a musician, naturalist, doctor, orator, teacher and friend. Only gradually, did it sink in that she was writing about me. Feeling humbled but wanting to share my discovery, I began to think: if my daughter could write about her feelings in such clear and glowing terms, so could every other child. Thus, the idea for this book was born. A collection of writings by children and young people about their most precious relationship - the one with their mother.

I set to work contacting children, asking for their help and then waiting for the response. When they came in their hundreds, I was overwhelmed.

I hope you enjoy reading it as much as I have enjoyed editing it.

Lynn Massey-Davis
1999

ADORATION

*"Most near, most dear, most loved and most far,
Under the window where I often found her
Sitting as huge as Asia, seismic with laughter."*

from *To My Mother* by George Barker

IT'S NO SACRIFICE

When she gets money for her birthday, she doesn't spend it on herself, she spends it on something that I need for me or my horse. I always tell her to treat herself but she never listens. My mother is so kind and unselfish, I don't know what I would do without her.

TARA, 14

She's always there when I have to go to the dentist - wretched brace! - and even takes days off work if I need my brace adjusted, taken off, or refitted.

LAURA, 14

When I am feeling worried about something or have doubts, she tells me that things will be alright and I feel better about everything. She listens to me too, when I am unsure. She's kind and caring.

ANON, 15

My mum doesn't give into me when I nag her to give me things. She reminds me of people who don't have anything. This makes me feel very proud of having a mum like her. She makes me think about things and I'm very proud of her for that. My mum wants me to be happy.

OLIVIA, 14

She's not fat and not thin, she's not small and she's not tall, sometimes she's sad but more often she's happy. She is my mum and I love her.

SAM, 14

My mum is caring, kind and loving because when I am in pain or sad, she hugs me and makes me happy again. Then when I am hurt she makes me better again.

BEN, 10

My mum is very special; she is also very funny. She lets me play with all of my friends and she tidies my room. My mum is the best mum. She may not be big but she is the boss.

XAVIER, 7

My mum is the best in the world because she brings animals home for me to love. She lets me go to my piano lessons but best of all she gives me cuddles. Could you wish for a better mummy? Thank you mummy for being kind to me this year.

IMOGEN, 7

SIMPLY THE BEST

The best thing about my mum is that she's always there when I need her. When I have a problem we sit and talk. Me and my mum get on well, sometimes we argue over silly things, but my mum and I have a lot in common.

NATALIE, 14

Your mother is the best thing in the world and you never want to let go of them even if they were to die. If my mother died I may as well die myself, because I wouldn't be able to carry on.

DAVID, 14

The best thing about my mum is that she brought me into this world and I could never live without her and she could never be replaced, ever!

ANON, 10

The best thing about my mum is that she's always there for me and understands when I feel sad or afraid. She's always interested in the day I have had and she supports me in any decision I make (within reason).

VICTORIA, 14

The best thing about my mum is her sense of humour. She is really funny. She comes out with these silly jokes and sometimes she tells corny ones which are not funny at all, but even then, I still love her.

JOANNA, 10

My mum is a very good listener and she understands when I am in a mood, happy or even hyperactive. She's very supportive and has always been there even when I have fallen out with everyone else.

GEMMA, 15

The best thing about my mother is her unwillingness to give up. She's very determined about everything she does.

ANON, 15

ON FRIENDSHIP

The best thing about my mum is the way she understands me and makes me feel more like a friend than a daughter. Even when we quarrel, my mum can always turn an argument into a joke.

LINDSAY, 14

My mother has a lot of good points but the best point about her is that she is always there for me when I need to talk about something and she is the only person I can show all of my feelings to. I always feel a lot better when I have spoken to her.

DAVID, 14

APPEARANCES

My mum doesn't have high heel shoes because she doesn't like them. She only likes flat shoes. My mum mostly smiles at me. My mum always wants to be like Mother Teresa.

DEBORAH, 11

I would say she has orange hair and is good-looking. She's also polite and helpful.

PHILIP, 11

I love my mum because she does my hair.

ABIGAIL, 7

MUM AS A TEACHER

My mum makes me feel really good when I get an award at school. She has always taught me to work hard and she has encouraged me to read from an early age, given me a love of poetry, art and nature which I will keep all of my life.

HANNAH, 14

BED TIMES

My mum's the best because she doesn't send me to bed until 9.00 o'clock and on weekends she doesn't send me to bed at all. When I sleep at my friend's house we have to go to bed **at 8.00 o' clock.**

BEN, 7

I love my mum because she lets me stay up till 7 o'clock and buys me Hartley's jam to eat. I love my mum very much.

GAVIN, 7

The best thing about my mum is that she reads books to me all of the time and she encourages me to do well at rugby.

JAMIE LEE, 10

What I like about my mum is that she plays with me and lets me stay up until 10 o'clock at night. She gives me hot chocolate at night as well.

RYAN, 7

BRING ME SUNSHINE

Even very young children, some aged barely five, and a couple with special needs wanted to write about their mums too.

My mum makes me happy when I go on my bike home.
                                HELENA, 5

My mum makes me happy when she takes me to work .
                                DECLAN, 5

My mum bought me a dog, called Suki.
                                SHANNEN, 5

Mum brought me a kitten called Jelly.
                                THOMAS, 5

Mum took me to see Nana.
                                SHARON, 5

My mum makes me happy when she takes me to granny Lucy's and granddad Ralph's.
                                ALICE, 5

My mum makes me happy by tickling me.
                                KIRSTY, 5

My mum made a special party for us with lovely balloons.
                                BEN, 5

EMBARRASSMENT

> "I never did, never did, never did like,
> 'Now take care dear,'
> I never did, never did, never did want,
> 'Hold my hand';
> I never did, never did, never did think much of,
> 'Not up there, dear!'
> It's no good saying it. They don't understand."

from *Independence* by A. A. Milne

As a mother of a 7-year-old, I now know the tricky tight rope my mother trod trying not to embarrass. Now my power to embarrass on all levels is blossoming of its own volition as I learn to say and do things to embarrass my children.

The quotes in this section show the full range of embarrassment, from A - Z, so be prepared to cringe.

My mum embarrassed me when she told her friends that I rode a pink bicycle and that I fell off it and started to cry. She also taped it on our camcorder and showed them what had happened.

DEAN, 10

DRUNK & DISTRESSINGLY DISORDERED

My mum always embarrasses me when she is drunk. She always hugs everyone and makes fun of me. When she's drunk, she can't walk straight at all.

LEWIS, 10

We were all having a laugh as a family, at a BBQ in our small village. My mum was getting drunk and started to chat some of the other men up. At 11.30pm, a camcorder was brought out and my mum was singing to ABBA. She was drunk and singing out of key. Then she got sloppy and tried to kiss us all. You should have seen her face the next day when the video was played on a large screen TV in the village pub.

JAMES, 14

My mum took a photo of me on my bike showing my bum. She enlarged the picture and hung it on my grandma's wall. When my friends go to my grandma's, my mum always shows the picture.

PHILIPPA, 9

My mum made me sing at the front of the church. This was embarrassing.

SUZI, 10

My mum can be a very embarrassing person. One time when I was six, and playing outside with a gang of friends, she came up to me in front of them and tickled me under my chin and said "Coochie Coochie Coo!". When she had gone, all of my friends started to laugh. I went bright red.

STACY, 11

My mum embarrasses me when she talks to her friends about me and I have to listen.

DANIEL, 11

My mum embarrassed me when she pulled my pants down in the street and slapped me on my bum.

STACY, 9

One time I went to watch a football match with my mother. When the fans were quiet, my mum shouted out loud and everyone looked around and stared at her. I did not want to be with her then.

DANNY, 14

SHOPPING FOR CLOTHES

Many mothers don't understand teenage fashions, and that people nowadays sometimes do pay just for a name! I believe that when a woman becomes a mother her purpose is not only to look after and care for her child, it is to embarrass them at every single opportunity especially when it comes to fashion and clothes!

TOM, 14

THERE MAY BE TROUBLE AHEAD?

When my mum got pregnant again, mum and dad took me and my sister out for the day. They told us about the pregnancy in a restaurant so that we couldn't shout at them. I was very pleased. My sister however, was very shocked and she made a joke about going to live with my granny and granddad until the baby was 21 years old.

HANNAH, 14

My mum sneezed in a shop and said, "Oh blast, every time I sneeze, I wet myself. I have had five children and have a very weak bladder." You could tell by the shopkeeper's face that as soon as we had gone he was going to laugh. I asked my mum why she had said this. I know it's a problem for her but she is too open about it.

LINDSAY, 14

I went shopping with my mum and sister. We looked in 20 shops, not one of which was my favourite army shop. I had to carry my mum's shopping back to the car. Worse was to come. When we were driving home we got caught up in a traffic jam. I was stuck in the back of the car having to listen to my mum's favourite song which is 'Money, Money, Money' by ABBA for two hours. I was very MAD!

WILLIAM, 13

JUST PLAIN DAFT

My mum can also be happy, like when we went to 'Pleasure Island Theme Park' she started running round in circles. I was quite embarrassed, but I could tell my mum was happy.

TRACY, 10

No matter how my mother may make me angry or embarrass me, I would never, ever be without her.

VICTORIA, 14

WHEN THE GOING GETS TOUGH

"The mother child relationship is paradoxical and, in a sense, tragic. It requires the most intense love on the mother's side, yet this very love must help the child grow away from the mother to become independent."

Erich Fromm, US psychologist and philosopher

As human beings we all have to deal with joy, tragedy and pain. Mothers somehow have to deal with their own feelings and ease the pain of others around them. Mothers are often the glue which holds the whole family together in times of stress.

Much of the supposed resilience of children comes from the knowledge that they are not alone. And in this knowledge, they grow.

When I was ill and had to go to hospital and stay, my mum stayed with me the whole time. I couldn't play with other children because they would catch what I had. She played with me all day. The baby next to us cried all night and kept her awake as she tried to sleep on a sofa bed next to me, but she never complained once.

HANNAH, 14

I am sad because my mum told me that Lee, my brother, has to go into hospital.

ROXY, 7

When a relative died, my mum listened to me and talked to me and explained why. She supported everyone in the family and put her own feelings on one side. A mother is someone who helps you understand all of the sad things which happen in the world.

LIZZIE, 15

When I was upset after falling out with my best friend, my mum asked me what was wrong. She listened and didn't say a word for a long time as I spoke for ages. At that point I realised I could tell my mother anything; I have ever since and she is always there when I need her. My mum is like my best friend and she makes me feel so proud!

CLAIRE, 14

When I ran away from home my mum was angry but calmed down after a few minutes. She then told me that she ran away but it got her no where and if I ever did it again she would not come looking for me. She made it sound real funny so that I would feel better. I then told her why I ran away and she helped me get over my problem.

KERRY, 14

When I was away for a swimming contest, my friend and me broke one of the rules. We were told we would be formally disciplined. I was scared at what my mum and dad would think. When I phoned my mum, I was in tears. She listened to my story and laughed. I couldn't understand at first, what she was laughing at. Then I laughed too. In this situation my mum showed me how to carry on through her support. It feels as if, when there is no one to turn to she's always there. I'm so proud.

TRACY, 14

IT'S A TOUGH JOB, BUT...

My mum is happy when she is doing the ironing.
When I come home from school she is happy.
BILLY, 7

My mum cleans. My mum tidies my room.

ASHLEY, 7

Mums should do anything you want. They should buy you anything you want from toys, shoes, to underarm deodorant.

RYAN, 9

My mum makes seeds grow in the back garden.

ABIGAIL, 7

ON EATING & FOOD

"Gave thee life and bid thee feed,
By the stream and o'er the mead;
Gave thee clothing of delight,
Softest clothing, woolly bright."

THE LAMB, by William Blake

Food is both the origin of conflict between mothers and their children and a potential source of joy.

Food and feeding came up a great deal in the writings submitted. Food rich in 'E' numbers and bright colours seems to win the day - a pure relief to mothers who believe they are the only ones waging the 'ketchup war' - phew! Jam and burgers rule OK!

FAVORITE THINGS

My mum is better at cooking than Ainsley Harriott!

CLARE, 9

The best thing about my mum is her bacon, sausage and egg sandwiches; they are simply gorgeous.

PASHA, 14

The best thing about my mum is her ability to prepare continental food like curries, Chinese, Italian etc. and the way she looks out for me.

JAMES, 14

My mum is the best mum in the WORLD!
My mum is the best cooker in the WORLD!
VICKY, 9

JAM ON IT

I like my mum, because she buys me Hartley's Jam and I love it. Hartley's jam is my favourite. Hartley's jam has strawberries in it and I love strawberry. Strawberry are my favourite.

ASHLEY, 7

I like my mummy because she gives me cookies and she gives me strawberry jam tarts. I like mummy because she gives me cakes. I like mummy because she takes me to a restaurant.

SEBASTIAN, 7

HOME MADE

My mum is good at cooking; she puts lots of meat in her home-made pies.

DIANE, 10

I hate it when my mum disguises broccoli and stuff in burgers and tricks me into eating vegetables.

ZOE, 7

I think the best thing about my mum is when she helps me bake lots and lots of buns. She lets me do lots of mixing but she doesn't let me put them in the oven in case I burn myself.

VIKKI, 9

She would spend her time cooking, just to make me happy.

MIRANDA, 14

My mum made me a chocolate cake for my birthday.

STACEY, 5

TEATIME SPECIALS

My mother's always busy
She's like a buzzy bee.
She always makes my breakfast,
My dinner and my tea.

SARA, 10

My mum cut some strawberry cake for me.

ANGUS, 5

My mum makes me happy when she gives me peas and sausages and chips.

KATIE, 4

She makes sure I have enough to eat and I have clean clothes.

SOPHIE, 9

My mum cares for me and she makes sure she gives me healthy food to eat.

SAMANTHA, 9

Mother, mother, the best in the world,
Cool, fab, funny, kind and wonderful,
And is good at all cooking you do?

CHRIS, 10

My mum gives me a red jelly for my birthday party.

HANNAH, 5

FLUFF 'N' STUFF

I love my mummy because she buys me hot chocolate. Hot chocolate is my favourite. My mum is nice to me because she buys me chocolate biscuits, which are my favourite.

ASHLEY, 7

My mum makes me happy when she buys me an ice cream.

DAMIEN, 7

I would say that mothers are sometimes nice and sometimes they are horrible and when you are good they buy you lots of sweets. Sometimes they are horrible and make you eat awful dinners and tidy your room.

MICHAEL, 10

DEFINING MOTHERS

> "Claudia...remembered that when she'd had her first baby she had realised with astonishment that the perfect couple consisted of a mother and a child and not as she had always supposed, a man and woman."

from *The Other Side of the Fire* by Alice Thomas-Ellis

Society continues to struggle with defining what a mother is. In grand explanations incorporating the sciences of biology, psychology and sociology whole texts have been written. In terms of defining responsibility of mothers, the linguistic perambulations of the law have also been well used. Not one of these wordy definitions encapsulates the essence of motherhood so well as any that follow here.

FROM FIRST TO LAST, ALWAYS...

If a woman has a baby, she is not a mother until she loves it. From the moment of birth to their last days together, motherhood is being the person a child will turn to in times of need. Adoptive parents can still be mothers if they love a child with as much love as they would give their own.

In the coldest, most scientific form of the word, a mother is a woman who carries and gives birth to a child. But it takes a lot more than that for a child to think of someone as mother.

LAURA, 14

If I had to define what a mum is, I would say: a mother is caring and kind, she should always be there for you whatever may happen. Mothers need to be good listeners and help their children if they get into trouble. Children should be able to trust their mothers and should be able to discuss things in confidence with them. Not all mothers are like this, but the least a mother should do is care for their children and put them first.

MIRANDA, 14

DRIVEN TO VERSE...
OR WORSE

My mum is exciting
And like most mums, hates fighting.
She's gentle and can be a bit mental.
We sometimes reach a compromise
And when she's suspicious
She looks into my eyes.

KYRIE, 10

My mum is kind. She is not nasty. She is not embarrassing. And she does not think she is too smart.

IMMY, 7

My mum is the best,
She's so much better than the rest.
She cooks, boils and fries my tea.
She does it just for me.
When I had a spider in my room
She barged in, killing it with a broom.

ADAM, 11

My mum,
She's the best that she can be.
My mum,
She's always good at organising me.
My mum,
She's as loving as can be.
My mum,
She's always understanding, for me
She's as generous as can be,
She's the best that she can be,
My mum!

LAURA, 15

SHORT AND SWEET

A mum is someone who gives you your name and your nature. She is cool, she is kind and she can read your mind.

JENNY, 11

The one thing you must remember is that though your mum might not always approve of what you do, she will always love you!

AMY, 14

A mother is someone who cares for you and protects you and keeps you safe.

VICTORIA, 14

WANTED: SOMEONE WITH SIX PAIRS OF HANDS

A mum is someone who gives birth to you and loves and protects you, looks after you, feeds you, and dresses you until you are old enough to do it for yourself. A mum is someone who buys your shoes and clothes and forgives you even if you do things wrong.

AMY, 12

My ideal mum would be someone who I could talk to, who wears the same type of clothes as me and has the same taste in music. Overall, she would be like my best friend!

GEMMA, 15

Your mother is your best friend, your advice giver, your helpline and your cuddly toy all rolled into one. She is someone you can always talk to and tell all your secrets to. Your mum will always get you out of a sticky situation, no matter what the consequences.

TARA, 14

A mother is someone who cares and loves you. A mother has to be kind and understanding and always ready to listen to your problems. She has to be quite strict, but not overprotective. If you need help, she has to be ready to help you.

MELISSA, 15

My mum says she never knew what love properly was till she had us. A mum wants to protect her children and keep them safe with every bit of strength she has, forever.

ELINORE, 16

AND GOD CREATED MOTHERS

And finally, the following piece was published in the *Home & Family Magazine*, the magazine of the Mother's Union, some time ago. I am indebted to them for publication of it in its entirety here:

When the good Lord was creating mothers he was into his sixth day of overtime when an angel appeared and said, "You're doing a lot of fiddling around on this one."

And the Lord said, "Have you read the specifications on this order? She has to be completely washable but not plastic...have 180 moveable parts, all replaceable. Run on black coffee and left overs...have a lap that disappears when she stands up...a kiss that can cure anything from a broken leg to a disappointed love affair and six pairs of hands."

The angel shook her head slowly and said, "Six pairs of hands? No way."

"It's not the hands that are causing me the problems," said the Lord, "It's the three pairs of eyes that mothers have to have."

"That's on the standard model?" Asked the angel.

The Lord nodded, "One pair that sees through closed doors when she asks, 'What are the children doing in there?' when she already knows."

"Another in the back of her head when she sees what she shouldn't but what she has to know. And of course the one in the front that can look at a child when he gets himself into trouble and say 'I understand and love you' without so much as uttering a word."

"Lord," said the angel, touching his sleeve, gently, "Go to bed. Tomorrow is another."

"I can't,' said the Lord, 'I'm so close now. Already I have one who heals herself when she is sick, can feed a family of six on one pound of mince and can get a nine year old to have a bath."

The angel circled the model very slowly. "It's too soft," she sighed.
"But tough," said the Lord excitedly. "You cannot imagine what this mother can do or endure."
"Can it think?"
"Not only think, but can reason and compromise." said the Lord.
Finally, the angel bent over and ran her finger along the cheek.
"There's a leak," said the angel.
"It's a tear."
"What's it for?"
"It's for joy, sadness, disappointment, pain, loneliness and pride."
"You're a genius," said the angel.
The Lord looked sombre. "I didn't put it there."

Acknowledgements:

Without the help and support of my friends, the children and young people from local schools, this book would not have been possible, so I would like to thank:

Endike Primary School in Hull, and the Head teacher, Malcolm Coates.

Patrington Primary School in East Yorkshire, and the Head teacher, John Bellwood.

Withernsea High School in East Yorkshire, and the Head teacher Martin Green and the Head of English, Jane Lodge.

Cottingham High School, East Yorkshire and Head of Science, Peter Smith.

And of course my own three, for inspiration: Imogen the beautiful, Tom the individual and the unstoppable Leonore, who is too young to write, except on walls.